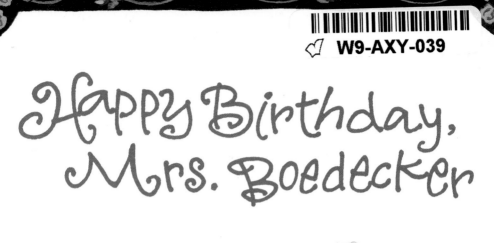
# Happy Birthday, Mrs. Boedecker

Written by Marcia Vaughan
Illustrated by Keiko Narahashi

CelebrationPress

*An Imprint of ScottForesman*

Ethan's favorite person in the world was Mrs. Boedecker. She lived next door.

Everything about Mrs. Boedecker was old: her house, her car, her clothes, even the way she wore her hair.

"How old is Mrs. Boedecker?" Ethan asked.

"She's as old as the hills," his father said.

"She's as old as the moon," his mother said.

"How old is she really?" Ethan asked again.

Nobody knew.

"How old are you?" Ethan asked Mrs. Boedecker as he pushed her around the garden.

"You will have to guess," said Mrs. Boedecker.

"My dad says you are as old as the hills," Ethan said.

"Close," Mrs. Boedecker laughed.

"My mom says you are as old as the moon," said Ethan.

"That's not too far off," Mrs. Boedecker said.

Ethan stopped pushing. "I'll tell you how old I am, if you'll tell me how old you are."

"That's fair," said Mrs. Boedecker.

Ethan stood up tall. "I am seven-and-a-half years old. I will be eight in July. Mom says I can have eight candles on my cake and invite eight friends to my party."

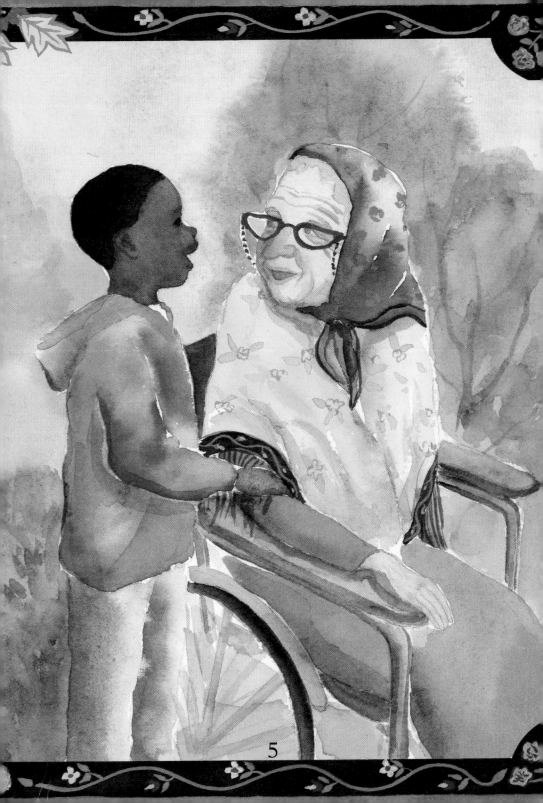

Mrs. Boedecker smiled. "I am ninety-nine years old. On my next birthday, I will be . . ."

"One hundred!" cried Ethan.

"That's right, Ethan," said Mrs. Boedecker. "When I was your age we always had pony rides on my birthday. Mama would make me a big cake with white icing and pink roses."

Ethan grinned. "This year you can put one hundred candles on your cake and invite one hundred friends to your party!"

Mrs. Boedecker stopped smiling. "Who would want to come to a party for an old lady?"

"I would," said Ethan.

Mrs. Boedecker reached out and hugged
Ethan. Her arms were very thin.

"You are my best friend, Mrs. Boedecker,"
Ethan whispered in her ear.

"You are my best friend too," she answered.

That night as Ethan lay in bed, he thought about Mrs. Boedecker turning one hundred without a cake or a card or a party.

Ethan made a list when he woke up the next day.

Monday
Talk to Bart, the baker
Tuesday
Call Grandma Pearson at the farm
Wednesday
See Mr. Gordon at the grocery store
Thursday
Visit Aunt Hazel at band practice
Friday
see miss Hossip at the newspaper

At noon on Saturday Mrs. Boedecker was pushing the last bobby pin into her hair when she heard a knock at her door. "Happy birthday, Mrs. Boedecker! Are you ready for a walk?"

"Yes, I am," said Mrs. Boedecker.

As Ethan wheeled Mrs. Boedecker outside, she looked around and smiled.

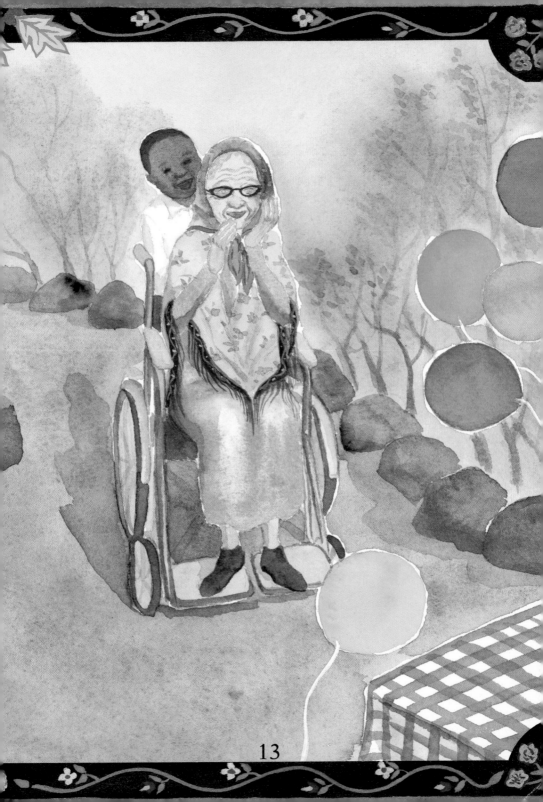

The garden was filled with people! Grandpa Pearson was setting up pony rides for the children. The Gordons were putting food on long tables. Bart the baker was putting pink roses on a big cake with white icing.

Mrs. Boedecker's face wrinkled with joy. "Did you do this?" she laughed.

"I did. And all your new friends helped too," said Ethan.

Before Mrs. Boedecker could say another word, Aunt Hazel raised her baton and the band began to play.

Happy birthday to you.

Happy birthday to you.

Happy 100th birthday, Mrs. Boedecker.

Happy birthday to you!